GOD IS SPIRIT

Brown Bear and Red Goose have two children, a gosling named Charity and a cub named John. They all believe in God.

God Is Spirit
2012

ISBN-13: 978-1480037625

ISBN-10: 1480037621

God Is Spirit

The Attributes of God for Children

One day Mama brought Charity and John to Papa with a question.

"Papa," they said, "What is God like?"

"That's a very good question!" said Papa. "Let's see what the Bible says about it."

Papa opened his Bible to the story about Jesus and the woman at the well. He read, "Jesus said to the woman, 'God is Spirit'" (John 4.24).

Charity looked up.
"What does that
mean?" she asked.

"It means God is like a person without a body," Papa explained.
"I don't get it," said John.

"Well, think of what happens to someone when he dies," said Papa.

"His body dies and is buried in the ground, but the person himself is still alive and goes to be with God. He can still think and feel happy. Even though his body is dead, the person is still alive without his body."

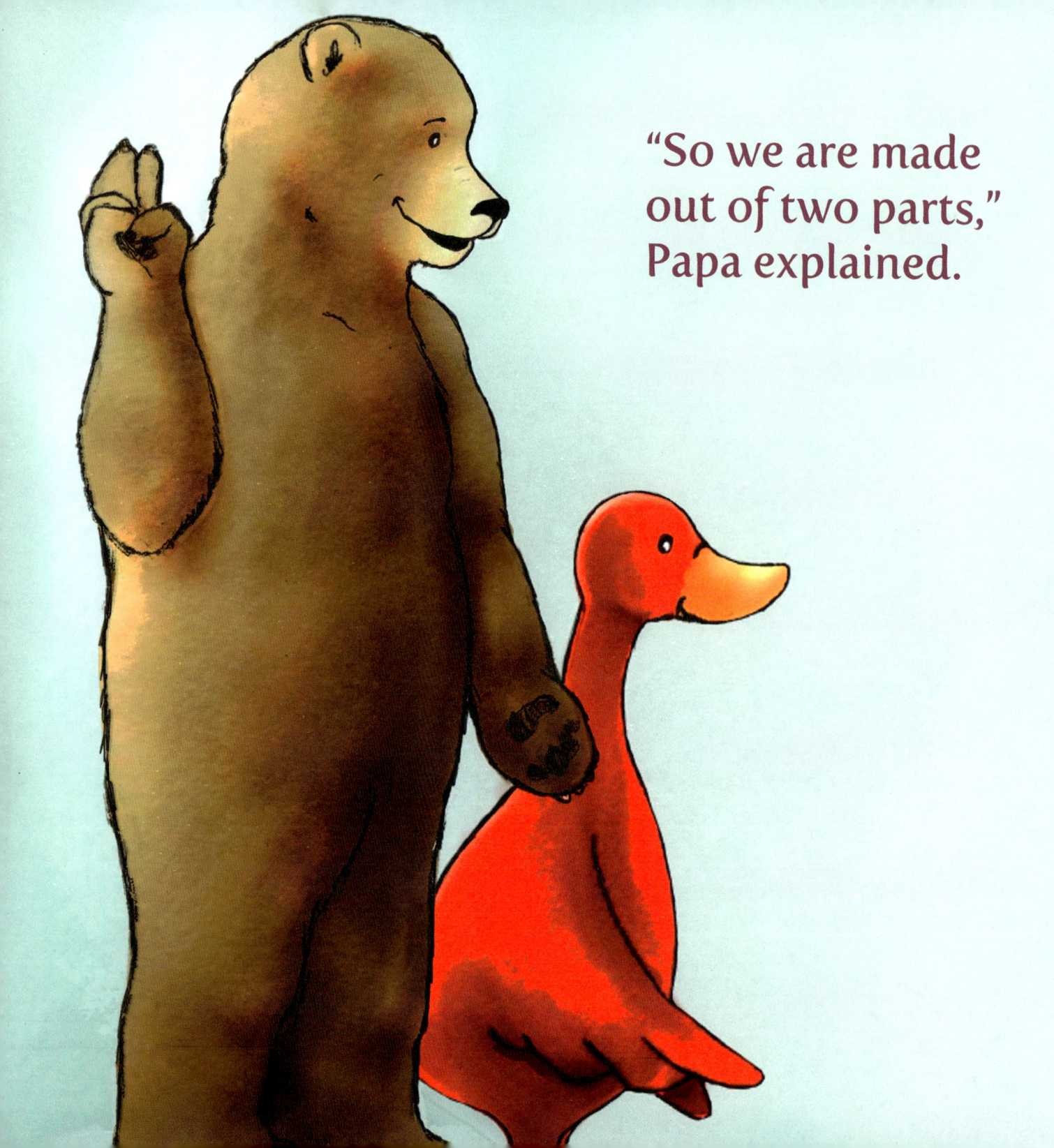

"So we are made out of two parts," Papa explained.

"One part is our body, which dies. The other part, which goes to be with God, is called our spirit. People are made out of a body and a spirit."

"But God is different," Papa said.

"You can't touch God because God doesn't have a body. Sometimes people think of God like an old man with a long, white beard. But that's not true. He is only spirit. That's why I said, 'God is like a person without a body.'"

"Is that why we can't see God?" said Mama. "That's right!" said Papa. "Since God has no body, we cannot see Him or touch Him."

"What else can we know about God because He has no body?" asked Papa.

"God can't get sick!" said John, "Or tired either!"

"That's right!" said Papa. I'm so glad you children are thinking about these things."

"It's fun to think about God!" said Charity and John. "We're going to think of more questions we can ask!"

Memory Verse:
"God is Spirit" – John 4:24

Books in the "What is God Like?" series

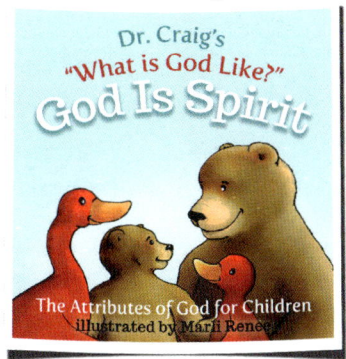

I. God is Spirit

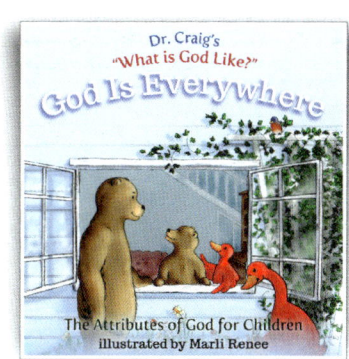

II. God is Everywhere

III. God is Forever

IV. God is Self-Sufficient

V. God is All-Knowing

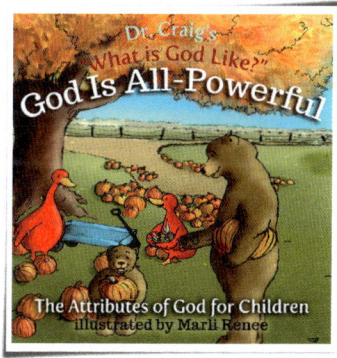

VI. God is All-Powerful

VII. God is All-Good

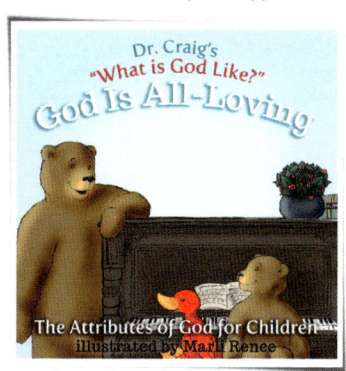

VIII. God is All-Loving

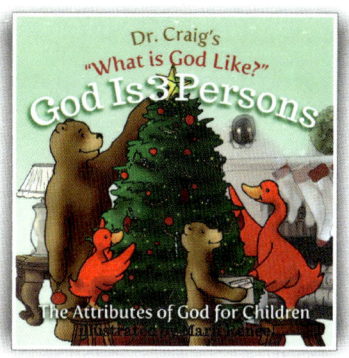

IX. God is Three Persons

X. The Greatness of God

"In these pages, you'll learn the most compelling arguments in favor of Christianity. You'll discover that *On Guard* is solidly factual, winsomely personal, consistently practical, and ultimately convincing in its presentation of the case for Christianity."

- Lee Strobel, former skeptic and author of *The Case for Christ* and *The Case for the Real Jesus*

ON GUARD

Defending Your Faith with Reason and Precision

WILLIAM LANE CRAIG

BEST-SELLING AUTHOR OF *REASONABLE FAITH*

Made in the USA
San Bernardino, CA
18 August 2013